I'm too busy to color!

The coloring book for adults who have real stuff to do

By Mike Artell

Published in the USA by MJA Creative, LLC

Box 3997 Covington, LA   70434

www.mikeartell.com

Public domain mandala artwork courtesy of Wikipedia Commons

Really? You have time to color?

Somehow, while most responsible grownups were busy at their jobs, raising their kids and trying to pay their bills, coloring books for adults became wildly popular.

Today's coloring books are supposed to provide stressed-out adults with a way to "unplug" and relax. But everyone knows that while they're sitting around playing with their colors, important stuff is not getting done. And it's piling up.

But a trend is a trend so let's do this. Here is a coloring book for adults who really have way too much other stuff to do.

Enjoy.

How to use this book

The left-facing page has instructions on what you should to do on the right-facing page.

If you become confused or are unable to determine what to do next, please don't vote or express your opinions on social media.

Color the facing page blue. Just use blue.

Color the whole page.

Ta-dah!

Color the white area inside each shape on the facing page. We've made the lines thick to save time.

Don't try to color the shapes on the next page. It will take too long.

Move on.

On the facing page is a color wheel for a color blind person. Color it using only gray and black.

Bonus time-saving tip: Don't feel pressured to stay in the lines.

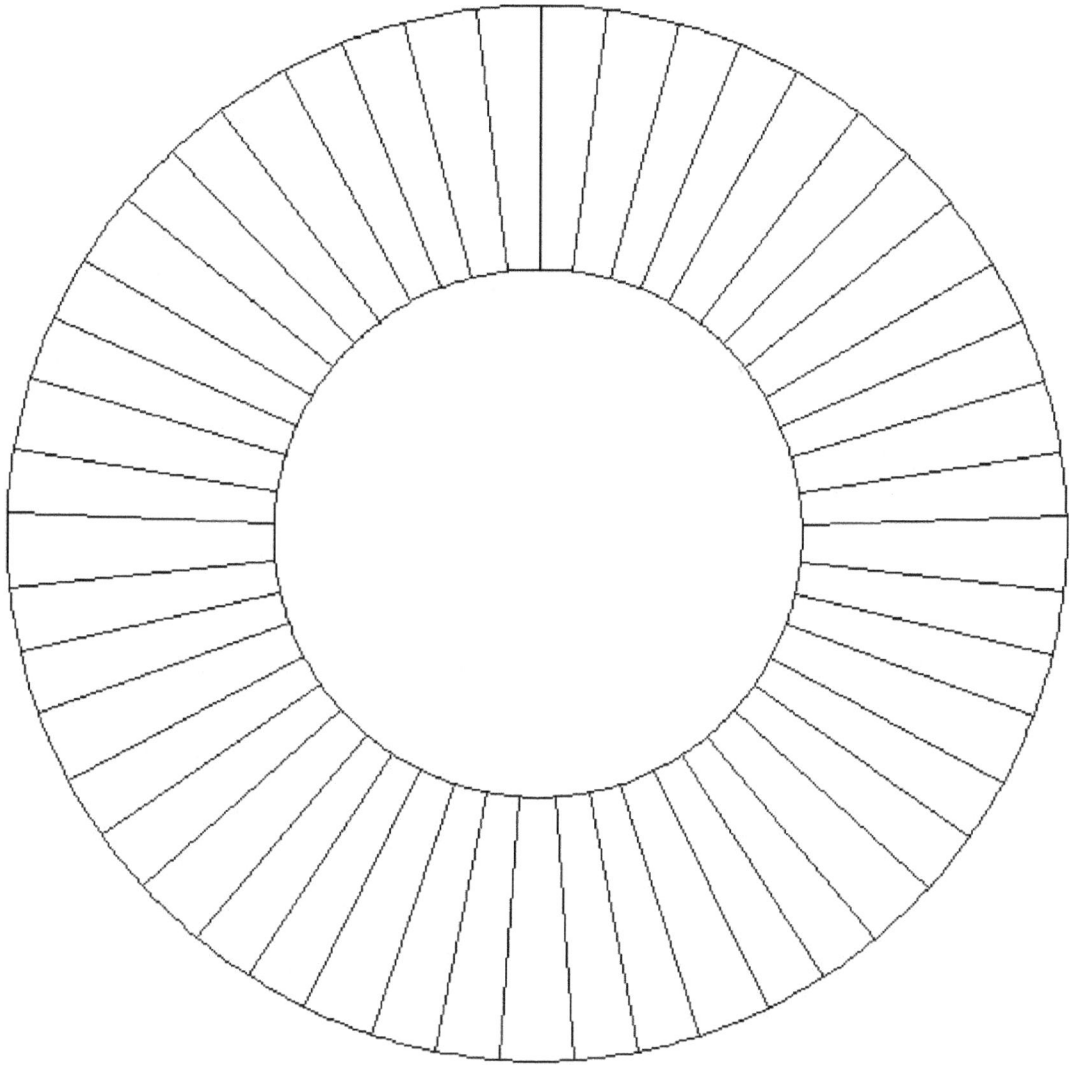

On the facing page use your crayon or colored pencil to list all the things you should be doing instead of coloring pictures.

You may use the last page of this book if you need additional space for your list.

Fill the facing page with multi-colored scribbles. Sign your artwork with the name, "Jackson Pollock." Frame your artwork and donate it to your local arts organization. Take a large charitable tax deduction when you file your taxes.

Take that useless white crayon out of the box. Use it to color the light gray shape on the facing page until it becomes pure white. Press hard.

When that fails (and it will) throw the white crayon away.

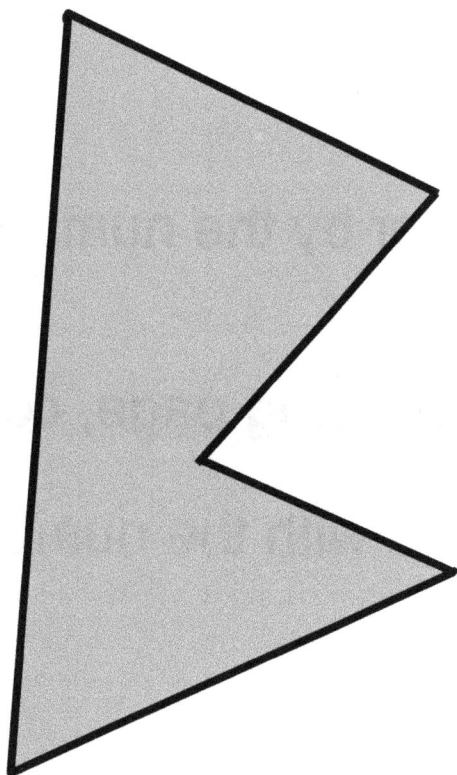

Color by the numbers

On the facing page, color all

the spaces with the number 5 red.

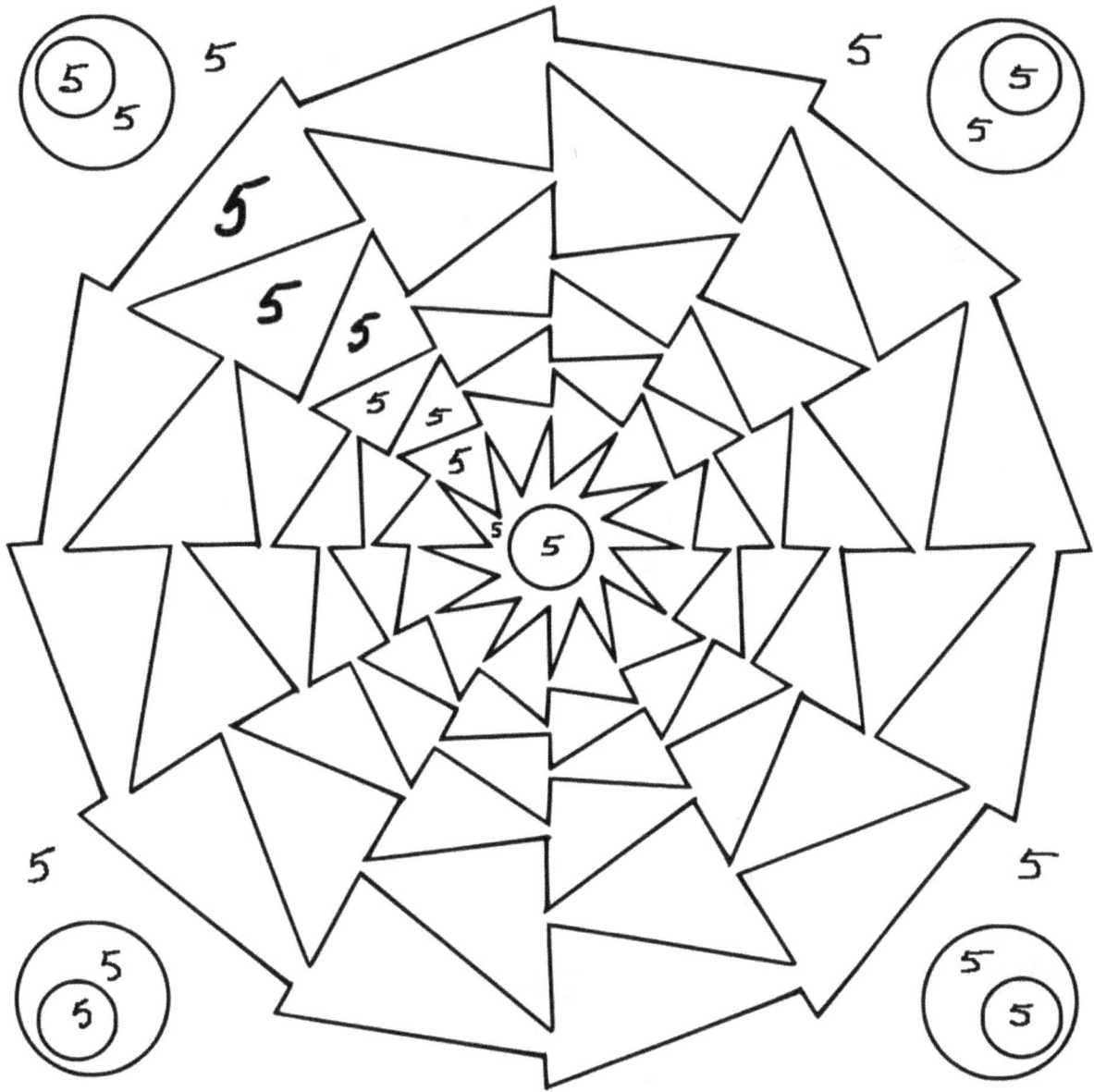

A mandala is a geometric figure that represents the universe. Or something deep like that.

Color each section of the mandala on the facing page a different color. Or one color. It doesn't matter.

Take a moment to admire the symmetry then quit goofing off and get back to work.

Color by the numbers (again)

On the facing page, color all

the spaces with the number 8 green.

8

The image on the facing page is a close-up of a snow drift. It's been pre-colored for you.

Move on.

Draw three random shapes on the facing page. Color each one a different shade of beige. Leave a lot of white space around the shapes.

Make a poster-sized copy of your artwork.

Sell it to a pretentious, boutique hotel as lobby art.

If your boss comes into the area while you're using this book, quickly cover this page with your left hand and leave the facing page showing.

EFFECTIVE DATE OF 1990 AMENDMENT

Pub. L. 101–549, title VII, §711(b), Nov. 15, 1990, 104 Stat. 2684, provided that:

"(1) Except as otherwise expressly provided, the amendments made by this Act [see Tables for classification] shall be effective on the date of enactment of this Act [Nov. 15, 1990].

"(2) The Administrator's authority to assess civil penalties under section 205(c) of the Clean Air Act [42 U.S.C. 7524(c)], as amended by this Act, shall apply to violations that occur or continue on or after the date of enactment of this Act. Civil penalties for violations that occur prior to such date and do not continue after such date shall be assessed in accordance with the provisions of the Clean Air Act [42 U.S.C. 7401 et seq.] in *effect immediately prior to the date of enactment of this Act.*

"(3) The civil penalties prescribed under sections 205(a) and 211(d)(1) of the Clean Air Act [42 U.S.C. 7524(a), 7545(d)(1)], as amended by this Act, shall apply to violations that occur on or after the date of enactment of this Act. Violations that occur prior to such date shall be subject to the civil penalty provisions prescribed in sections 205(a) and 211(d) of the Clean Air Act in effect immediately prior to the enactment of this Act. The injunctive authority prescribed under section 211(d)(2) of the Clean Air Act, as amended by this Act, shall apply to violations that occur or continue on or after the date of enactment of this Act.

"(4) For purposes of paragraphs (2) and (3), where the date of a violation cannot be determined it will be assumed to be the date on which the violation is discovered."

EFFECTIVE DATE OF 1977 AMENDMENT; PENDING ACTIONS; CONTINUATION OF RULES, CONTRACTS, AUTHORIZATIONS, ETC.; IMPLEMENTATION PLANS

Pub. L. 95–95, title IV, §406, Aug. 7, 1977, 91 Stat. 795, as amended by Pub. L. 95–190, §14(b)(6), Nov. 16, 1977, 91 Stat. 1405, provided that:

"(a) No suit, action, or other proceeding lawfully commenced by or against the Administrator or any other officer or employee of the United States in his official capacity or in relation to the discharge of his official duties under the Clean Air Act [this chapter], as in effect immediately prior to the date of enactment of this Act [Aug. 7, 1977] shall abate by reason of the taking effect of the amendments made by this Act [see Short Title of 1977 Amendment note below]. The court may, on its own motion or that of any party made at any time within twelve months after such taking effect, allow the same to be maintained by or against the Administrator or such officer or employee.

"(b) All rules, regulations, orders, determinations, contracts, certifications, authorizations, delegations, or other actions duly issued, made, or taken by or pursuant to the Clean Air Act [this chapter], as in effect immediately prior to the date of enactment of this Act [Aug. 7, 1977], and pertaining to any functions, powers, requirements, and duties under the Clean Air Act, as in effect immediately prior to the date of enactment of this Act, and not suspended by the Administrator or the courts, shall continue in full force and effect after the date of enactment of this Act until modified or rescinded in accordance with the Clean Air Act as amended by this Act [see Short Title of 1977 Amendment note below].

"(c) Nothing in this Act [see Short Title of 1977 Amendment note below] nor any action taken pursuant to this Act shall in any way affect any requirement of an approved implementation plan in effect under section 110 of the Clean Air Act [section 7410 of this title] or any other provision of the Act in effect under the Clean Air Act before the date of enactment of this section [Aug. 7, 1977] until modified or rescinded in accordance with the Clean Air Act [this chapter] as amended by this Act [see Short Title of 1977 Amendment note below].

"(d)(1) Except as otherwise expressly provided, the amendments made by this Act [see Short Title of 1977 Amendment note below] shall be effective on date of enactment [Aug. 7, 1977].

"(2) Except as otherwise expressly provided, each State required to revise its applicable implementation plan by reason of any amendment made by this Act [see Short Title of 1977 Amendment note below] shall adopt and submit to the Administrator of the Environmental Protection Administration such plan revision before the later of the date—

"(A) one year after the date of enactment of this Act [Aug. 7, 1977], or

Watch for Mike's new book coming soon!

Here's a sample page from the next book in this series:

I'm too busy for dot-to-dot!

Connect the dots. Level 1.

1
●

2
●

Mike Artell is the author of more than 40 books, most of which he also illustrated. Every year, Mike visits more than 50 schools across the U.S., Europe and Asia where he shares his techniques for thinking, writing and drawing more creatively with thousands of students and teachers.

For more information about Mike's books, videos and personal appearances visit mikeartell.com. You can also find Mike's cartooning videos on YouTube (search "Mike Artell") and you can follow Mike on Twitter @mikeartell.

www.ingramcontent.com/pod-product-compliance
Lightning Source LLC
Chambersburg PA
CBHW081235020426
42331CB00012B/3179